Welcome to the world of Funky Winkerbean!

Funky's just an average guy, trying to cope with High School, love, a summer job, and more than a little help from his friends.

They're all here: Crazy Harry, Marcia and Jan, Les, The Coach and many more. Add quips from a crazy computer and the wacky "wisdom" of the "I Chong," and you've got PLAY IT AGAIN, FUNKY. Sometimes hip, always hilarious—Funky's fun for everybody!

PLAY IT AGAIN, FUNKY!

By Tom Batiuk

tempo
books

GROSSET & DUNLAP, INC.
Publishers • New York

For Cathy

YOU KNOW, 'CRAZY'... BREAKING UP WITH A GIRL HAS TO BE THE HARDEST THING IN THE WORLD TO DO!
I WOULDN'T AGREE WITH THAT, FUNKY!
BATIUK
9/18
THE HARDEST THING IN THE WORLD TO DO IS TOUCH YOUR NOSE WITH YOUR TONGUE!

SAYINGS FROM THE
I CHONG
ANCIENT BOOK OF CHINESE PHILOSOPHY

THE MASTER SAYS: IF YOU WISH TO KNOW TRUE BEAUTY, SEEK OUT A BEEKEEPER WITH A BEE IN HIS LEFT HAND ...

FOR BEAUTY IS IN THE EYE OF THE BEE-HOLDER!

SAYINGS FROM THE
I CHONG
ANCIENT BOOK OF CHINESE PHILOSOPHY

FOR A GOOD TIME THESE DAYS
YOU SHOULD FIGURE ON SIX
YEN AND UP!

IT IS BEST NOT TO GO OUT
INTO LIFE WITH A YEN FOR
PLEASURES OF THE FLESH!

SAYINGS FROM THE

I CHONG

ANCIENT BOOK OF CHINESE PHILOSOPHY

THE MASTER SAYS: THERE IS MUCH TO BE LEARNED BY SITTING NEXT TO A RUSHING STREAM AND LISTENING TO WHAT IT TELLS YOU!

UNLESS, OF COURSE, YOU'RE SITTING NEXT TO A BABBLING BROOK!

CRAZY HARRY IS GOING TO LISTEN TO 'MY SWEET ANGEL' AT FULL VOLUME UNTIL HIS SPIRIT TRANSCENDS THE PHYSICAL WORLD!

HAS ANYTHING HAPPENED SO FAR, LES?

YEAH, HE'S HAD THREE NOSEBLEEDS!

BATIUK

© Field Enterprises, Inc. 1973

1-31

BATIUK

7-29